Figuring in the Figure

Because design, alone, doesn't hold weight,/" Ben Berman writes in his remarkable second collection of poems, "we need concrete material—the image/ of a bridge over the sound of water." In *Figuring in the Figure,* Berman explores the nature of form in its deepest most complex sense, how it sustains and protects us, how it allows us a kind of freedom within its restraints, but how "even stable/ structures that are well designed and built/ with integrity are susceptible/ to fractures." His luminous details evoke a world of mutable forms and shapes that suggest the fragility of our lives. In poem after poem, he demonstrates his mastery of terza rima, moving in, out and around the form with his playful diction and subtle music. The book culminates with a moving, realistic yet lyrical sequence of poems about the birth of his daughter. This is a quietly beautiful book that deserves attention and recognition.

—Jeff Friedman, author of *Pretenders*

Figuring in the Figure is a self-portrait of a man becoming a father. Ben Berman writes inside a modified terza rima that makes a virtue out of clarity and discernment. The influence here of Frost is hardly fashionable, but certainly sincere and Berman returns us to Frost's virtues: these poems make points and have a point of view. Like Frost, Berman is unsparing in his introspection. He offers us an ongoing philosophy: when faced with the pain and contradiction of everyday life, "to delay judgment and contemplate . . . incompatible thoughts."

—Rodger Kamenetz, author of *The Jew in the Lotus*

B en Berman's nimble terza rima is the perfect vehicle for the poems of *Figuring in the Figure*. Both expansive and structured, the interwoven stanzas allow him to form and reform probing questions of identity without ever forsaking a deep musicality. There are tremendous powers of observation on display here. We watch the speaker ponder mouse droppings, hit the wall in a marathon, describe the great molasses flood of 1919, diaper a doll in a birthing class, then try to manage his "tiny fascist" of a toddler who wouldn't stop until "every bookshelf toppled/ like a/ failed coup." His observations are enriched with various kinds of humor—aphorisms, riddles, word plays, and puns. This book is wise and wonderful.

—Beth Ann Fennelly, Poet Laureate of Mississippi,
author of *Unmentionables*

B en Berman's fine, clever poems are never merely clever. Their frisky formal play is finally and importantly about the finding of forms that might adequately contain our feelings. As his title, *Figuring in the Figure,* suggests, Berman is fond of double meanings; indeed, he is in love with all the twists and turns of language, as well as all the structures that display the pleasures of thinking. If invention is his inclination, order is his learned yet sly companion, "a partner," he writes, "the type/ that coyly invites chaos to dance."

—Lawrence Raab, author of *Mistaking Each Other for Ghosts*

FIGURING
in the FIGURE

POEMS BY
Ben Berman

ABLE MUSE PRESS

Copyright ©2017 by Ben Berman
First published in 2017 by

Able Muse Press

www.ablemusepress.com

Printed in the United States of America

Library of Congress Control Number: 2016956288

ISBN 978-1-927409-71-8 (paperback)
ISBN 978-1-927409-72-5 (digital)

Cover image: "In the Lattice" by Alexander Pepple

Cover & book design by Alexander Pepple

Able Muse Press is an imprint of *Able Muse:* A Review of Poetry, Prose & Art—at www.ablemuse.com

Able Muse Press
467 Saratoga Avenue #602
San Jose, CA 95129

For my parents,
who somehow offered me both roots and wings

Acknowledgments

I am grateful to the editors of the following journals where many of these poems originally appeared, sometimes in earlier versions:

New Haven Review: "After the Epiphany"

Pedestal: "Shifting Centers"

PoetryNet: "A Familiar Form" and "After Installing the Safety Gate"

Raintown Review: "Figures"

Rattle: "The Underside"

Redactions: "Droppings"

Salamander: "Nothing Archaic about It" and "Re Form"

Solstice: "The Great Molasses Flood"

South Hampton Review: "Arch Poetica" and "Origin Story"

Third Wednesday: "Wrestling with Angles"

Unsplendid: "Homeric Nods," "Loose Ends," and "Takeoffs"

Contents

III

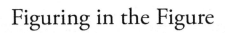

Figuring in the Figure

I

The artist must value himself as he snatches a thing from some previous order in time and space into a new order with not so much as a ligature clinging to it of the old place where it was organic.

— Robert Frost (from "The Figure a Poem Makes")

Wrestling with Angles

I used to think corners were the least edgy
things around—show me the tightest of lines
converging and I'd see the frame of a cage.

And those figures haunting the suburbs—trimmed lawns,
file folders, tennis nets with their rows
of right angles and their upright columns—

lacked any meaningful depth. I wanted raw
forms—the tangled coils of intestines,
say, being scavenged by ravenous crows,

or winding rivers and those untrusting
steps sideways on jagged, uneven rocks.
But a body can only stand so much twisting

and turning—a back twinges, a knee locks,
and soon we think of mountains as scenic
landscapes to display on our desktops,

learn that even orderly and secure
shapes are mere facades—think of an EKG,
that flat line on a rectangular screen.

The Underside

My friend tells me how his wife cheated—
well, not cheated, but sent racy photos
of herself to other men—how she created

some online profile with a phony
name, *Lady Falcon,* and how he stumbled
upon this one day when he used her phone

to order pizza. They'd been so stable,
he tells me, maybe they needed this breach
to save their marriage from growing stale.

In front of us a hawk is perched on a branch,
calmly pecking at a squirrel's entrails.
We're sitting side-by-side on the bench

but see different things through the tangled
crosscutting of limbs in front of us. My friend
mentions that he'll hide some of the details

from his analyst because the man can find
subtext even when they chat about sports,
which makes me feel bad about my own feigned

attention, how my mind spirals and spurts
like a squirrel getting chased up a tree,
then scrambles to piece together the excerpts—

it's just that I'm tired of the puppetry . . .
my friend says . . . *some childhood desire . . .*
he adds . . . *while residing on my property . . .*

But what an impotent word—*reside*—
no wonder why his wife sent all those nude
pictures to random men. On the underside

of the branch, now, directly under
the hawk is another squirrel, his floppy
tail pointed stiff. This must be *duende,*

I think, ready to spring at the slightest flap
of a wing. *How should I have reacted?*
my friend asks, as the squirrel fixes to flip.

Origin Story

The sky couldn't have been more glorious—
pinks and purples above the dark ocean—
but my sights were set on all the girls

who weren't talking to me as I sipped my can
of stale, lukewarm beer, worried that the flat
taste on my tongue would forever contain

me, that I was destined to always flirt
with the idea of flirting. My eyes stung
from all the smoke that had begun to float

my way and though it was suffocating
to sit by that fire, taunted by the dance
of those flames, I soon found myself staring

at a lone ember and the radiance
of its self-possessed glow, how it burned
without some burning need for audience.

Still, it wasn't until the cute blonde
beside me placed her hand on my thigh and warned
me not to stare too long lest I go blind

that I realized the allure of wonder,
the quiet power of turning inward.

Droppings

It might be the crumbled ash from a match,
I tell myself, *or toasted seed from a loaf*
of multigrain bread. But my stomach

seems to already know that there is life
behind the walls—something about the pinched
ends. No different, say, than the slightest lift

in my wife's voice—that imperfect pitch—
that tells me she's upset long before she tells
me she's upset. And it's always when speech

and language are barely a tail's
length apart that we dwell on those gaps
and what's behind them—each tiny trail

leading to something just out of our grasp.

After the Epiphany

In the movie, a streak of lightning transformed
the sand into delicate glass figurines—
as though all it takes is a thunderstorm,

as though all that intricate filigree
adorning the glass was the mere result
of some sudden flash. But real fulgurites,

it turns out, look more like mangled roots—
opaque and grainy—about as glamorous
as their name. Not to praise the realists

who see the light but speak only of glares,
wander through this world without wonder,
but how often we see things as clear as glass

then crash, like birds, into some window.

Merging Courses

We'd read about the farm-to-table fad
and signed up for one of those kitchen tours
where you can follow the path of your food,

and though we witnessed the inside story—
walked past the display of liquor cases
and wine coolers to face the chilling stares

of hundreds of hanging carcasses—
we still somehow believed that the sublime
and vulgar never fully merged courses,

still distinguished that succulent leg of lamb
from all of those bloody, severed limbs.

The Game

Matopos, Zimbabwe

The jungle, to us, was this big carnival
where you could shoot photos of gnus
snuggling with their adorable calves,

but our cameras must have looked like guns,
and those wildebeests stopped grazing on ferns
and began instead to snort and moo and grunt.

Still, not until one hunched down on all fours,
lowered its gangly mane and then charged
did we see not furry but fury,

realize the game had suddenly changed.

Grit Theory

We tried counting steps and adjusting our form,
closing our eyes and pretending the ground
was the ocean and we were flakes of foam,

we chanted our mantras, grunted and groaned,
convinced ourselves blisters were first-world
problems and that grit would come from the grind.

But by mile twenty, we'd hit a brick wall,
found ourselves running on mortared joints,
learned just how quickly a hardened will

can transform into a rigid won't.

Figures

In

It's better to figure things *in* than *out,*
to delay judgment and contemplate
instead a few more incompatible thoughts,

allow all the various and competing
narratives to coexist, see each one
as completely right but not complete.

Drawing

It is not the breast that we focus on
but the shadow the breast casts over a fold
of flesh—the kind of attention we only

achieve when we allow our minds to follow
thoughts rather than think, when we detach
ourselves in order to feel more fully.

Heroic/Tragic

How often we see their lives and deaths
as connected but not conflated,
like those panels of a Warhol diptych

that hinge on the notion of twofold
truth, portray even the most iconic
of idols as divided and faulted.

Of Speech

Perhaps they're only fanciful conceits,
witty schemes and stylistic devices,
but there's something about sound in concert

with sense that changes our sense of a voice,
transforms basic conveyances of thought
into grand, luxurious vehicles.

Compulsory

It's not just about skating the perfect eight—
the restraint of edge control and even flow,
command of inward curves and shifts of weight—

but how often our greatest leaps follow
our strictest attention, as though constraints
and freedom made perfect bedfellows.

Significant

The challenge is counting only what counts
then saying something of measured value
that acknowledges the uncertainty

of our tools, stresses the prevalence
of doubt—how hard it is to pinpoint
anything other than our ambivalence.

Legends

Unlike the deceptive nature of fine print,
writing a caption involves the challenge
of taking a picture and trying to paint

a clearer picture—an art that belongs
to science, the kind of invaluable
practice that only takes place in legends.

Ground

The figure and ground grow reversible
when you walk down the street with a child.
How quickly the formerly invisible

path transforms into a wonderland of chewed
gum and strewn leaves, while that house where a meal
awaits begins to look like a passing cloud.

Out

Just when we fear that we're destined to mull
things over without ever landing upon
a solution, we end up taking a small

step sideways, shift our original plans,
realize we just might be able to count
those angels if we find different-shaped pins.

II

The line will have more charm for not being mechanically straight. We enjoy the straight crookedness of a good walking stick.

— Robert Frost (from "The Figure a Poem Makes")

The Great Molasses Flood

Here and there struggled a form . . .
Only an upheaval, a thrashing about
in the sticky mass, showed where any life was.
— The Boston Post, *1919*

Over two million gallons of molasses
turned Boston into a modern Pompeii,
drowning men and horses under massive

waves, a surreal disaster prompted
by the thick syrup's rising internal
pressure, which rattled the tank and popped

all of its bolts loose. The initial
reports blamed the distilling company's lack
of oversight—found they had installed

the tank in a hurry, camouflaged leaks
by painting the sides brown and used steel
that was far too thin even by the lax

standards of the day. But even stable
structures that are well designed and built
with integrity are susceptible

to fractures, not because they're too brittle
to withstand the stress from heavy loads,
but from tensions within—the very word, *bolt,*

meaning both *to lock down* and

break loose.

Arch Poetica

Because design, alone, doesn't hold weight
                we need concrete material—the image
of a bridge over the sound of water.

Often, we don't even notice the bridge
                unless it draws our attention as it draws
down. Until then, we think only of passage.

When we walk along an arcade, we're drawn
                not to the frame but to what the frame
opens—those portals that lure us inward.

Here, the aesthetics are meant to perform
                specific functions, and the structure,
though related, is different from the form.

And yet, everything is connected—construct
                a solitary, stand-alone tower
and even that goes back to the Etruscans.

Takeoffs

Travel the same path enough times and you
forget it's a choice, forget even the most
trivial of decisions were at one point

fraught with uncertainty, until say, coming
home from a trip, you miss your connecting
flight and some woman at the bar calls you

handsome. And even though it has been years
since you've sipped brandy at an airport,
humored some dead-end flirting, sometimes the

essence of a story is in how it
begins, not ends—that charged opening
scene that leads nowhere, those questions

begging to stay questions—which is why when the
pilot says to prepare for takeoff, you
bring your seat forward, attentive to the

preflight routine, smiling as that woman
pleasantly explains how to go down in flames.

Loose Ends

Sometimes, both senses of *refrain*—
to stop and *to repeat*—hold their stances
like kung fu stars in some poorly dubbed foreign
film.

And often the run-on sentence
is less a mistake than a thought that's overly
complete; lines spoken after the scene
has finished.

It's a never-ending volley—
a poem clicks, says Yeats, *like a closing box;*
a poem's never finished, says Valéry,
only abandoned.

It's why, when someone breaks
up with us, we suggest staying friends—
hearing the ride is over, hoping the brakes
won't work.

Gap Years

We graduated with degrees of doubt,
feared committing   but we were worried,
                                  too, that our travels would disorient

ourselves to careers when the very word,
contract, reminded us   us even further,
                        that we'd fly to the other side of the world

of the constricting grips on our futures,
and all those dotted lines   and end up sitting
                        around complaining about all the rifts

awaiting our signatures felt like signs
of incomplete paths;   and disconnects,
                  as though they were just part of some grand design.

Homeric Nods

There's a difference between letting scraps
stew and making a pot of diluted
trimmings.

And yet how often our scrapes
with danger come so neatly dovetailed
with the mundane—
                         our car spins on black ice
and all the big abstractions and small details
swirl together: terror and fuzzy dice,
reverence and the latest catchy pop tune
on the radio.

But this is the price
we pay for thinking of *united*
and *tangled* as long-lost distant cousins
with a striking resemblance to some aunt
that neither has ever met.

Cézanne's
the father of us all, said Picasso,
who used geometric shapes—curves and cones,
cubes and spheres—to break figures into pieces.

But how do we claim a legacy
when it's hard enough to connect process
to product,
                    content to form,
                                    when logic
excludes more than it connects?

                                At best, we're bound
to feel gratuitously nostalgic
for the way our mothers turned beef bones
and celery hearts into stew—

                        how complete
they made us feel back then with those balanced,
wholesome meals perfectly filling our plates.

Re Form

Not starting from scratch but with a scratch
of certain measures.

***

              Think of the voltage
lurking behind the simplest of switches.

***

Best to be charged by—not with—violating
a rule.

***

       Long after the rush of new paths
comes the enduring delight of traveling
old paths in new ways.

***

              There are turns in patterns,
a seed in proceed.

***

       We cannot defy
traditions until we treat them as partners.

***

Grapple with time and space, modify
timing and spacing.

***

       Adopt and *adapt*
have different senses of fidelity.

Not quite free rein but like a droplet
bounded by free surfaces.

We proceed
with the double mind of a diplomat.

Both meanings of *forgo*—*to precede*
and *relinquish*—must find ways to cross
paths.

Sometimes, *fixed* doesn't mean prescribed
but improved.

A dead form is like a carcass
that makes the richest of stocks.

Think of freedom
and tradition as opposite charges.

If form's *an extension of content*, reform
must be an extension of discontent.

All living forms are destined to morph,
and each slight mutation leads to distinct
species.

***

The secret is in merging notes
of dissent into lines of descent.

***

Even a word as certain as *definite*
is a stress away from *defiant*.

***

Fragments,
too, seek their own form of narrative.

***

Every custom needs a custom frame.

***

We must test just how far we can stretch
our ideas before they lose all sense of form.

***

Going Home Again

Travel the world and you'll feel most distant
                                    upon
                        returning to
            where you
are from,
embody that same sense of disconnect

you feel when you see yourself on film
                            and think
            but that's
        not even
my voice,
or find yourself dating a former

lover with some outdated version
                        of yourself,
            lost and
disoriented,
as you try to drive forward in reverse.

Transformations

Set a story somewhere and your setting
takes on a life of its own, emerges
as a landscape, the kind of subject

that requires complete immersion.
Before you know it, your story is both
in and of the mountains, portrays images

behind the action and the meaning beneath—
those cliffs portending a steep decline,
fauna conveying hopeful signs of rebirth.

***

***

Declining nouns was as fun as cleaning
chalkboards and left an equally dry taste
in our mouths. I'd always joked about cloning

myself and subjecting *him* to my testy
teachers. Then, one day in detention, my friends
wondered aloud if I never protested

because *I* was the clone. How foreign
my distaste for translation suddenly felt,
so much waiting to be redefined.

***

***

Felt isn't woven. It's pressed until flat,
until each fiber has snagged and matted
and all those individual filaments

have intertwined, forming a material
whose uses couldn't be more various—
piano hammers, knee pads, yurts, marker-tips.

Still, there's something to fabrics that serve
a simpler purpose, rely on a single strand,
the slightest fray and it all unravels.

***

***

Stranded, for Thoreau, meant time to transcend
society—he didn't just walk alone
in the forest for hours, he *sauntered,*

believing his strolls would lead him *à la
sainte terre.* There was something about the woods
and fields, in particular, that allowed

Thoreau to *feel free from all worldly
engagements,* as he'd set off for that point
of no return, his mind yielding to the wild.

***

***

Point to a flower or faraway planet
and a baby will stare at your finger
as though pointing, itself, was the point.

And because language is always referring
us elsewhere, we find ourselves liable
to forget how textured and foreign

words can be—until a baby babbles
as she reaches for our hand and the notion
of elsewhere suddenly feels unbearable.

***

***

Notions were spread on the table like nations
at war—pins, stitch rippers, needles—work tailored
for folks who can devote their full attention

to the present task. But every detail
presented me with an escape, a means
to imagine spools spilling their entrails

all over the desk, scissors as Siamese
twins. And the more I tried to focus, the more
the thread spun wildly from reel to seam.

***

***

Mores is one of those words that's morphed
to join the ranks of *pluralia tantum*—
like any of us who've gotten married

and begun living our lives in tandem
with others. Just recently, I complained
to my wife that we never spend any time

alone. By *alone,* I meant as a couple.
On nights when she's away, I order
takeout. Even when full, I feel incomplete.

***

***

Order, too, is worthy of great odes—
not the classifying, or numbering,
or reducing feelings to the idea

of feelings, or those painfully numbing
times when we believe in right answers,
celebrate compliance, equate naming

with taming, or praise the work of ants—
but order as a partner, the type
that coyly invites chaos to dance.

***

***

Type down some loose thoughts and soon you're tapping
away at the keys as though your hands
could unlock what's been stuck on the tip

of your tongue for years, as though your head
could transform from a noun into a verb—
the mind abuzz with all those meanings hidden

somewhere within. I want to live on the verge
of my ideas—all of my beliefs set
in stone, stones waiting to be turned over.

***

III

The figure is the same as for love . . . and ends in a clarification of life—not necessarily a great clarification . . . but in a momentary stay against confusion.

— Robert Frost (from "The Figure a Poem Makes")

Birthing Class

Breaking the Ice

We're split in two and asked to discuss our hopes
and fears, though my group mostly shares our unease
with being labeled *The Moms' Helpers.*

It is not until our partners unleash
their response—*the pain, the pain of being split
in two*—that we feel the distance between us.

Light Touch Therapy

When the nurse encourages us to spoil
the moms, I whisper, *You're like a cup
of bad milk.* Seeing us laugh, the nurse slips

over to my wife. *Jokes might help you cope,*
she tells her, *but don't be afraid during
transition to tell him to cut the crap.*

We Practice Changing

I'm not sure how many more doll-diaperings
are in me, or clips of birth I can endure.
But just as I feel my blood sugar dropping,

I look over at my wife and some inner
voice begins to kick in, reminds me, *Forget
what's in you and focus on what's in her.*

PacknPlayCarSeatDiaperCreamBreastPumpNippleBrushBabyTubBouncySwing

As though trapped on some long, domestic flight
the dad-to-be beside me unscrambles
words in his book of puzzles, fidgeting

with letters, trying to reassemble
some sense of order—as though we could practice
navigating our way through the shambles.

You Can Cut the Cord if You Want

The cartoon in the back of the packet—
a potbellied man handing out cigars—
serves as an ironic, dated picture.

But I wish it felt even more incongruous,
that while my wife's body surges with life
I could do more than support and encourage.

Form and Aesthetic Distance

My wife bonds with the other moms as I fill
out forms. But as I watch her from my seat
all of my qualms almost begin to feel

right, as though when your role is to assist—
to help something bigger than you take shape—
a little distance can be a great asset.

After Installing the Safety Gate

A single screw pokes out of the wall
like a tiny erection, stripped so hard
all we can do is hope that it will

fall out on its own, its slotted head
smiling like some obnoxious clown,
so now I, too, feel stripped, my manhood

uncloaked in yet another unclean
finish to a project, as though I'll always
be the wandering, eccentric uncle

of my own home, the shame of my halfway
commitments exposed in the front hallway.

Expecting Fathers

It's just warm enough so that the snow banks
on our street are both gushing and stoic
at the same time. If we attribute the brink

of seasons to Demeter's ecstatic
joy, then perhaps these false spring days could
belong to us—with their easing of strict

airs and thaw of such a tightly packed cold.

L'Dor Vador

For my grandmother, who died a few hours
after my daughter was born.

She would have claimed that God was granting
us a deep and spiritual bond, one final
connection between generations.

But for the next few days I'd be folding
monkey blankies and thinking of shrouds;
felt almost giddy at the funeral

when I saw distant cousins and shared
my good news. My heart would suddenly throb
and I couldn't tell if I'd just shuddered

with grief or joy or a tangling of both,
everyone whispering their *congrats*
and *condolences* in the same breath.

The Art of Parenthood

After Henry James

It's one thing to know a route by heart,
another to know it with your mind,
and I'd never truly feared the threat

of getting stuck in one of those midday
delays until we strapped my daughter
into her tiny bucket seat and my mild

neuroses exploded into deranged
visions of precarious paths pregnant
with every conceivable danger—

falling acorns pelting us with portents,
traffic signals flashing their red alerts—
as we clutched the wheel as new parents,

those people on whom nothing is lost.

Nothing Archaic about It

After Rilke

She wakes and cries out with an onslaught
of needs, beckons us like the torso
of Apollo: *You must change your daughter.*

And to hear her tempestuous throes
as we fumble with the snap of her buttons
is to realize how easily change throws

us all off balance—these tattered patterns
of sleep, our quarters cramped into eighths,
the relentless demand to put down

our work, books, forks—not that it doesn't feel right,
but the *right* in *right now* is intensive.
Our ends have never felt so loose. The tight

fit of our best swaddle is tentative
in the fits of her sleep. Even on weekends
we're up before three. Something has to give.

But we hold on—holding her—tired, weakened.
And something else inside of us awakens.

Roots and Wings

There are only two lasting bequests
we can hope to give our children.
One of these is roots; the other wings.
    — *Hodding Carter*

You can only hush and hum for so long,
rock and cradle so much, before you're ready
to admit that your newborn's not nuzzling

into your chest but rooting at your dry
nipple, before you reluctantly pass
her to your wife and take over the laundry,

wondering what it would be like to express
your letdowns, to just let them flow freely
from your body, instead of all the repressed

whimpers you make when your daughter falls
asleep and you step on those windup
chattering teeth and have to flail

about like an upturned tree in the wind,
your roots flapping so hard they look like wings.

A Familiar Form

We'd hoped that some tiny bits of solid
food would lead to a solid night's rest,
deliver us from the piles of soiled

onesies, but mixed fruits had mixed results,
ground meat always wound up on the ground,
and she somehow mistook chunks of roasted

squash for miniature hand grenades.
She'd protest the texture, reject the flavor
or simply start gagging, and all our grand

dreams of order would come crashing to the floor,
which is why we almost started to rejoice
when, changing her, we found a familiar

form, like *umeboshi* on a bed of rice,
with its perfect sense of calm and grace.

Shifting Centers

I

It's just after the crocuses emerge
that the temperature always
                        seems to drop—
the seasons weathering their rocky marriage—

and now a late winter storm has disrupted
the first week of spring, and
                        drifting patches
of snow and sleet have turned the front doorsteps

into a slide. How I would have looked past
this once, simply shoveled,
                no wide-eyed toddler
leading me to reimagine these paths.

II

She lies between us like a tendril,
coiling   winding
     and   between   fixed
                    two   sides,
and it's always when we have just trailed

off to sleep that she begins to slide
and   and
   flip   turn   a
          like   geometry
problem gone wrong, then spins like a spitted

pig, flaps about like a lost migratory
bird—   fast
    both   asleep   the
              and   fastest
shapeshifter in all of mythology.

III

She toddles around like a tiny fascist,
ready to knock
                down whatever
we've built,
attacking our structures with open fists,

until every stack of blocks has been bulldozed,
every bookshelf toppled
                    like a
failed coup.
She searches each room for anything balanced

then pulls on it until it's on the cusp
of falling down,
                    as we learn to bear
the brunt,
pray that things will survive their collapse.

IV

We pass our daughter like a baton,
and as our hands touch
                during the exchange,
it's clear that something has come between

us, as though successfully executing
such teamwork requires
                coming together
without colliding, as though the exacting

art of a marriage teeters between the tight
coordination of
                opposing motions
and seeing each other as moving targets.

V

I have forgotten what it once meant
to hear   the word idle   as ideal,
to sit quietly chanting a mantra

or spend the morning playing with ideas
without feeling   like something   is wrong.
Now, I suggest another round of hide-

and-seek so that I can vacuum the rug.
Dust dances   in a beam   of sunlight
and I reach immediately for a rag.

VI

My daughter won't eat a broken saltine,
cut up   or quartered
          potato,   grape.
She likes things intact, demands solutions

to the slightest dissolution, wants to grip
the whole   she can   pronounce.
               of what   partially
Rejecting my fractured vision, she groups

all fragments together—draws pictures
on paper   dances when a
               and walls,   truck backs
up, builds towers out of puzzle pieces.

VII

Set my daughter inside a cardboard box
                              and she'll sit
in it all morning just reading her books

or diapering Elmo or trying to shift
                    gears on her plane,
reinventing that empty space to suit

her imagination, lost in that open-
                              ended
play of creating new worlds with her pen.

VIII

Because basic tasks feel like great endeavors,
these days, I decide to   wait
until naptime to head out on my errands.

But no one in line coos, or smiles, or wants
to overhear   me sing
quietly to myself, no one stops to watch

me sneeze—it all feels so meaningless,
every   empty
exchange a reminder of what's missing.

IX

She stands in middle of the room, attempting
to jump,   flapping her arms like   branches
                                                    the
of a tree possessed by a tempest,

laughing wildly as she bends and bounces,
leans and lurches,   staggers   shuffles.
                                    and
And as we watch her throw herself off balance,

launch into this frenzy of constant shifts,
it's as though we're being   made in   image,
                                                her
renewed by the ever-transfiguring self.

Ben Berman's first book, *Strange Borderlands* (Able Muse Press, 2013), won the Peace Corps Award for Best Book of Poetry and was a finalist for the Massachusetts Book Awards. He has received awards from the New England Poetry Club and fellowships from the Massachusetts Cultural Council and Somerville Arts Council. He is the poetry editor at *Solstice Literary Magazine* and teaches in the Boston area, where he lives with his wife and daughters.

Also from Able Muse Press

William Baer, *Times Square and Other Stories*

Melissa Balmain, *Walking in on People – Poems*

Ben Berman, *Strange Borderlands – Poems*

Michael Cantor,
    Life in the Second Circle – Poems

Catherine Chandler, *Lines of Flight – Poems*

William Conelly, *Uncontested Grounds – Poems*

Maryann Corbett,
    Credo for the Checkout Line in Winter – Poems

John Philip Drury, *Sea Level Rising – Poems*

D.R. Goodman, *Greed: A Confession – Poems*

Margaret Ann Griffiths,
    Grasshopper – The Poetry of M A Griffiths

Katie Hartsock, *Bed of Impatiens – Poems*

Elise Hempel, *Second Rain – Poems*

Jan D. Hodge, *Taking Shape – carmina figurata*

Ellen Kaufman, *House Music – Poems*

Emily Leithauser, *The Borrowed World – Poems*

Carol Light, *Heaven from Steam – Poems*

April Lindner,
    This Bed Our Bodies Shaped – Poems

Martin McGovern, *Bad Fame – Poems*

Jeredith Merrin, *Cup – Poems*

Richard Newman,
    All the Wasted Beauty of the World – Poems

Alfred Nicol, *Animal Psalms – Poems*

Frank Osen, *Virtue, Big as Sin – Poems*

Alexander Pepple (Editor),
    Able Muse Anthology

Alexander Pepple (Editor),
    Able Muse – a review of poetry, prose & art
    (semiannual issues, Winter 2010 onward)

James Pollock, *Sailing to Babylon – Poems*

Aaron Poochigian, *The Cosmic Purr – Poems*

John Ridland,
    Sir Gawain and the Green Knight – Translation

Stephen Scaer, *Pumpkin Chucking – Poems*

Hollis Seamon, *Corporeality – Stories*

Carrie Shipers, *Cause for Concern – Poems*

Matthew Buckley Smith,
    Dirge for an Imaginary World – Poems

Barbara Ellen Sorensen,
    Compositions of the Dead Playing Flutes – Poems

Wendy Videlock,
    Slingshots and Love Plums – Poems

Wendy Videlock,
    The Dark Gnu and Other Poems

Wendy Videlock, *Nevertheless – Poems*

Richard Wakefield, *A Vertical Mile – Poems*

Gail White, *Asperity Street – Poems*

Chelsea Woodard, *Vellum – Poems*

www.ablemusepress.com

CPSIA information can be obtained
at www.ICGtesting.com
Printed in the USA
BVOW03s0036021216

469571BV00001B/13/P